D0887772

HumanStory

Human History from the Dawn of Time to the Dawn of the New Age.

By Ron Logan and Michael McClure

NUCLEUS Publications
Willow Springs, Missouri

HUMANSTORY
Human History from the Dawn of Time to the Dawn of the New Age
by Ron Logan and Michael McClure

Copyright © 1989 by Ron Logan and Michael McClure. All rights reserved.

Published by NUCLEUS Publications, Rte. 2, Box 49, Willow Springs, MO
65793. Send for free catalog.

Library of Congress Cataloging in Publication Data

Logan, Ron.
   HumanStory: human history from the dawn of time to the dawn of the new age.
by Ron Logan and Michael McClure.
     p.   cm.
   ISBN 0-945934-01-7 : $8.95
   1. World history—Humor. 2. Social history—Humor.   I. McClure,
   Michael, 1950—   . II. TITLE.
   D23.5.L64 1989
   902' .07—dc20   89-27959
                                                          CIP

Printed in the United States of America

Dedicated to P. R. Sarkar

Introduction

History is communicated in a culture according to the collective psychology of the times. Homer composed his saga of Greece's Trojan War, and Vyasa his narrative of India's Mahabharata War, using the medium of the epic poem and interlacing mythological tales with historical events. Gibbon in *The History of the Rise and Fall of the Roman Empire*, and Toynbee in *A Study of History*, wrote within the tradition of Western rationalism and gave scholarly accounts of history. Engels and Marx, during a period of revolutionary foment, presented their dialectical view of history in the form of a manifesto.

There has been an evolution in the way humans attempt to grasp reality. This was the great insight of Swiss cultural philosopher Jean Gebser, who made a monumental study of the evolutionary development of human consciousness. Gebser perceived that the cognitive styles humans have used to understand their world have evolved from magical to mythological to mental (mental in the sense of rational). Gebser believes that human consciousness is now undergoing another fundamental shift, from the rationality of the mental style to an emergent arational structure of consciousness. Characteristic of arational cognition is its integrative, holistic, non-linear and intuitional nature. This is the style of consciousness which will become dominant in the new era, the era which social commentators have variously called post-industrial, post-modern, aquarian, or new age. We can already see the prevalence of this patterning of thought among people identifying with new age culture and holistic paradigms.

Prabhat Rainjan Sarkar has given a theory of history which, in content and mode of expression, is compatible with this new age structure of consciousness. His body of thought covers a wide range of disciplines, but he does not come from the tradition of academic scholasticism. His teaching is in the tradition of the sage. Like the Buddha and Ramakrishna, he has presented his philosophy in inspired oral discourses. But, unlike past sages who spoke almost exclusively of the perennial philosophy, of spiritual and moral concerns, Sarkar has stepped into the intellectual territory of scholars and is propounding original socio-economic and scientific theories.

In his discourses on history, Sarkar portrays the pattern of human events in broad, intuitive strokes. He draws more on archetypal imagery than on historical documentation to convey his theory. His narrative is vividly expressed and rich in humanistic moral judgment. Here, for example, are some of Sarkar's comments on the oppression of women during the Medieval Era, when an ecclesiastic elite dominated society:

The [clerical intelligentsia] reduced women to the position of wageless slaves. Conspiring to cripple women in every way, they fabricated "divine" commandments together with numerous kinds of scriptural injunctions, paralogical tenets, and imaginary yarns of sin and virtue. . . The majority of women became mere objects of enjoyment. Society refused to recognize anything except their ability to conceive and bring up their progeny. . .

In the first dawn of human knowledge, women, too, imparted knowledge to others. They also composed mantras and offered libations to the sacrificial fires sitting beside men. In the [Medieval] era, however, they lost that role, and all possible means were taken to firmly establish their slavery. . . Women were relegated to the status of animals and cattle. They became mere household necessities. . . Few keep count of the millions of women who wept and sobbed themselves to death in the darkness of many a sleepless night. They were leveled flat like soft earth under the administrative steam-roller of the [intelligentsia].

This is not an account of the Middle Ages from the dispassionate tomes of the scholarly historian. This is history told with reference to the experience of the human heart.

In writing my brief synopsis of Sarkar's theory of history, I felt it appropriate to preserve his descriptive style, using accessible and vivid imagery rather than obscure and dry historical fact, and adopting a narrative rather than analytical flow of thought. To complement and accentuate this writing style, Michael McClure has illustrated the text in a comic fashion, using archetypal images familiar to a Western audience. His graphics highlight important concepts and add lightness through frequent juxtaposition of humor with the text's intense, epochal depiction of history.

HumanStory is an introduction to Sarkar's ideas on the dynamics of history, central to which is his concept of the social cycle. To appreciate the significance of the social cycle, it is helpful to review the perspective Sarkar has taken on causality in history. The attempt to identify the causal agent behind historical dynamics has been a central concern of historians. Marx believed that economic forces of production generated antagonistic class differences which led to successive forms of class struggle. His notion of historical causality was firmly rooted in dialectics and philosophical materialism. Spengler held the view that the life of a nation is analogous to the seasons of the year: a people's history goes through its vigorous springtime assent, its robust summer flowering, its autumnal decline, and its winter decay and death. In Spengler's naturalistic interpretation of history nations, like physical organisms, must suffer inevitable demise. For Toynbee, the genesis of a civilization results from a people's making a creative response to a challenge presented by their natural or social environment, with its continued existence contingent on its ability to meet fresh challenges. Thus, for Toynbee, the historical process is rooted in the human spirit; material and naturalistic forces only present the adversity to which human fortitude must respond.

Sarkar analyzes history from the perspective of collective psychology. He builds his view of historical causality primarily upon human personality archetypes and their expression in collective aggregates. Sarkar identifies four personality archetypes, which, in their collective expression, form four psycho-social classes. These are: the laborers, whose primary activity is physical toil; the warriors, who are engaged in physical challenge; the intellectuals, who are involved with mental pursuits; and the capitalists, whose concern is with economic enterprise. Each of these archetypal personalities has—as explained in more detail in the text—their own characteristic style of self-expression.

Now we come to Sarkar's concept of the social cycle. For Sarkar, the natural pattern of history involves the cyclic rotation of these psycho-social classes into positions of social dominance. The natural progression of the social cycle occurs in the following order of class dominance: from laborer class to warrior class, to intellectual class to capitalist class. Attaching this natural cyclic order to human history, we find that the early and middle Paleolithic era was dominated by the laborer class, the upper Paleolithic era and the Age of Antiquity by the warrior class, the medieval era by the intellectual class, and most of the modern era by the capitalist class.

The second rotation of the social cycle began with the workers' and peasants' revolutions of the 20th Century which brought the warrior class into dominance for the second time. In Eastern Europe, we are now seeing the beginnings of the transition from militarist dominated societies to new social orders dominated by the intelligentsia. This transition from the second warrior era to the second intellectual era validates the prediction Sarkar made when he first propounded his social cycle theory in the late 50's. Sarkar rejected Marx's idea that a classless society would evolve following the overthrow of capitalist class dominance. He held instead that communist societies are dominated by the militarist class, and that this militarist class would eventually be succeeded by the rise of the intellectual class. Recent events in Eastern Europe and the Soviet Union substantiate Sarkar's theory.

Theories of history are ordinarily of interest only to students of history. Marx, Spengler and Toynbee are exceptions, their ideas having attracted a wider audience. The principle reason that Marx's historical materialism, Spengler's rise and fall of nations, and Toynbee's genesis of civilizations command so much attention is that these historical theories provide powerful perspectives with which to analyze and predict currents in human affairs. They are used to make the case for the necessity of class struggle, for the fated decline of the American empire, or for concerns over the lack of a spiritual vitality in Western civilization.

As evidenced by the social cycle's capacity to shed light on the historical dynamics at work in Eastern Europe, Sarkar's theory of history carries this same sense of relevance. But Sarkarian history has a relevance with goes beyond its apparent predictive validity. Its greater importance is its appeal to those compassionate souls who seek to understand history so they can effectively move a human society in crisis onto a new course, a new destiny. Sarkar asserts that spiritually aware and humanistically dedicated people—a classless group he calls *sadvipras*—can guide the movement of the social cycle in a manner that will largely eliminate the historical scourge of class oppression. In Sarkar's opinion, it is one of the great tasks of this transitional era in human history to establish sadvipran personalities in nuclear positions of influence in society. If this were accomplished, universal human interests would surpass class interests in the affairs of society. Sarkar makes this final appeal in *Human Society II*, his treatise on history:

The social cycle shall go on and on. None can stop this rotation. . . one era always follows another. The sadvipras cannot stop this process. [But] they must be vigilant so that. . . [class interests] do not become exploiters but govern society as benevolent leaders. . . In the absence of a sadvipra society the social cycle is moving on its natural course. In every age the leadership of the predominant class has become exploitative, and thereafter comes evolution or revolution. For want of sadvipras' assistance, the foundation of human society is lacking firmness. . . These sadvipras shall work for the good of all countries, for the all-round emancipation of the entire humanity. The downtrodden humanity of this disgraced world is looking to the eastern horizon, eagerly awaiting their advent with earnest zeal. Let the cimmerian darkness of the interlunar night disappear from their faces. Let human beings of the new dawn wake up in a new world.

Two decades ago, humanity was able to look at its world from a new perspective. Through the eyes of the Apollo astronauts we saw our home planet as one world floating in the vastness of space. This view has stirred us to recognize that our world is inhabited by one indivisible humanity. We now see awakening in our collective consciousness a new mythos: that of universal humanism. A vision of history is now needed which illumines and vitalizes humanity's conversion to universal humanism. Sarkar has met this need; he has given us an aquarian view of history.

Ron Logan

Chapter One

The Era of the Laborer

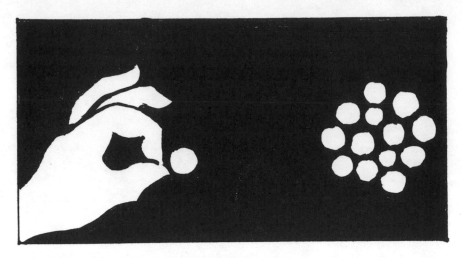

Out of the unfathomable Cosmic Imagination . . .

. . . our universe was conceived and born.

In an enormous explosion, elemental energies and particles emerged from the void and were hurled outward into the vastness of space . . .

Matter clustered to form stars, and stars were gathered into great swirling galaxies.

Our sun—one star among billions in the Milky Way galaxy—became the hub of a planetary system. Our earth, situated a favorable distance from the sun, possessed the right conditions for complex molecules to form.

Three billion years ago, somewhere in the primordial muck which covered the earth's surface, life began.

Several million years ago the erect-walking, communal, intelligent primate Australopithecus emerged.

From Australopithecus evolved Homo erectus, with the dawning of human-like consciousness.

Then came Homo sapiens with new powers of mind, including the capacity to create culture and civilization. So began the human story.

The first expression of humanity's social existence was far from noble. There was little to distinguish human life from the life of other primates.

Prehistoric humans faced a hostile environment. Powerful predatory animals, inclement weather, and the hard labor of hunting and gathering food made their lives a continuous struggle for survival.

The minds of early humans were preoccupied with meeting their physical needs— there was little scope for higher pursuits. This created in them a laborer mentality, and shaped the nature of their society.

These prehistoric laborers were not guided by high ideals or by human values. They acted in response to the immediate demands of their environment, and their society was formed accordingly. They lived in small groups, maintained out of a mutual need for self-protection and division of labor.

Within these groups there was no established social order; neither were there fixed social ties. Group and family bonds were weak. Their harsh existence gave them little scope to feel closeness or to express sympathy towards the frail and the suffering.

Mating relationships had little permanence and were typically polyandrous. Family ties arose from the sentiment mothers developed for their children.

The lives of the early laborers were filled with hard physical toil, leaving them with little opportunity to use their minds creatively.

Their culture reflected the nature of their existence. Their art portrayed sensual or material concerns.

Religious feelings arose out of their fears.

They attributed supernatural powers to the awesome forces of nature, which they dreaded and could not comprehend.

For thousands of years, prehistoric humans toiled and struggled in their unglamorous existence. But gradually, out of this harsh and difficult life, a new type of mentality evolved.

A few within the laborers' society ceased to face the world with submissiveness and fear. They began to look upon the obstacles and dangers of their environment as challenges to boldly confront and conquer.

To express their conquest-loving mentality they developed new, warrior-like character traits: courage, spiritedness, and valor.

Those with a warrior mentality became a distinct new class, and rapidly rose to dominate the more fearful and submissive laborers. Society underwent a metamorphosis to a warrior society. The late Stone Age marked the beginning of the warrior era.

Chapter Two

The Warrior Era

Early warriors lived to express valor and vitality through fight and conquest.

Because of their high-spiritedness, they developed a strong sense of honor. In battle, they would not strike a person from behind, nor would they attack the young or helpless.

The warriors' code of honor held more importance to them than their existence. They preferred a noble death to ignoble defeat or dishonorable conduct.

Their concern with prestige caused a sense of conscience and duty to awaken in them. This had a healthy effect on society; out of duty, the warrior men began to take greater responsibility for their families.

Women no longer were burdened with being the sole providers and protectors of the young . . .

. . . and socially-recognized marriage came into vogue.

At the beginning of the warrior era, the system of leadership was matriarchal. Brave and spirited women were recognized as group mothers of the clan or tribe. This early matriarchal rule was humanity's first expression of an established social system.

Gradually men's role in family life became more prominent. This led to a decline in the status of the group mothers, and matriarchy was eventually replaced by the rule of male chieftains and monarchs.

Although women no longer were the leaders of the society, they still enjoyed a social status equivalent with men's and were respected as men's equals.

The warriors remembered and glorified the valiant deeds of their ancestors. Tales of the heroic exploits of their forebears gave them the inspiration to boldly undertake new risk-filled ventures.

Because of the respect instilled in them for their family heritage, warrior children developed a sense of duty towards their parents and family ties became very strong.

With the formation of tight family units, society too became more firmly united.

Unlike the laborers, the warriors' religious expression was not motivated by fear of the forces of nature. The warriors' religion reflected their fearless, high-minded mentality. When they prayed, they asked their gods to provide for the subjects under their rule. Their deities were usually powerful animal spirits or human-like gods and goddesses who possessed qualities glorified in the warrior society. There were high points of religious expression in the warrior age, including the inspired teachings of Pharaoh Ikhnaton, the lyrical praise of God by King Solomon, the mystical yoga of the Pandava princes, and the taoist wisdom of King Wen.

Because of its warring nature, the warrior society required a high degree of social unity and firm social discipline.

There was also a need to bind kingdoms together with an efficient system of social administration and to coordinate the building of means of transport and communication. It was in the warrior era that the state came into being.

When the warrior society became patriarchal, leadership was held by a chieftain who established his right to rule by virtue of his superior physical might.

Whoever in the tribe proved himself to be the strongest commanded the respect and authority to lead the clan.

With the death of a chieftain, the strongest warriors would battle each other to establish a successor.

To put an end to the destructiveness of these conflicts, a hereditary system of succession began, and monarchy came into vogue.

Because of the power and daring of the great warriors, most people looked upon them with fear and awe.

They willingly submitted to the warriors' rule . . .

. . . and often attributed godlike status to them.

The kings, in turn, felt an obligation to protect the subjects under their dominion.

But the reign of these absolute monarchs was not always paternal and benevolent. At times they maintained their dominance in a brutal and rapacious manner, callously wielding power for the sake of their own vainglory.

Their subjects became cannon fodder in their incessant wars of plunder and conquest. They lusted after ever-increasing glory and dominion, and built up their empires without concern for the toll of lives lost in battle.

With hereditary succession to the throne, reign was often passed on to unworthy descendants.

Such descendants became monarchs by virtue of their birth, but they lacked the true warrior qualities of heroic bravery and high-spiritedness.

These pseudo-warriors eventually came to predominate the royal families. The weakening of leadership in the warrior society foreshadowed the fall of the warrior class from their position of unchallenged dominance.

The warriors had physical strength and courage, but they lacked the intellect needed to devise subtle tactics of warfare or to invent sophisticated weapons. They needed the help of people with intellectual skills.

On their own, they could not administer their increasingly complex, expanding kingdoms. In the process of building up their empires, the warriors became more and more dependent upon advisors.

In the latter part of the warrior era, continuous military clashes and ever-growing transportation, communication and administration problems created conditions for the growth of a class of people engaged in intellectual work.

Not only did the number of the intellectually employed increase, but their designs on power also grew. The dull-witted, pseudo-warrior royalty simply could not fathom the wiliness of the aspiring intellectual class.

The ministers of the court filled their monarchs' ears with flattery and praise—and then proceeded to tell them what to think.

Almost unawares, the proud and regal royalty had their formidable power wrested from them by shrewd administrators and councilors.

The duped kings became puppets to their ministers, and the system of rule was no longer that of monarchy, but became a "ministocracy."

While the locus of power shifted, the outer form of government did not change. The ministers who held the power behind the throne maintained the facade of monarchy. In this way, they could conveniently control the commoners who had accepted that their kings ruled by virtue of divine right. A new era dawned in human history, one in which society was dominated by the intellectual class.

Chapter Three

The Intellectual Era

In the early phase of the intellectual era, society benefited to some extent from this change. The intelligentsia introduced a more orderly social system.

They often saved the common people from the monarchy's arbitrary high-handedness and from the cruel slavery to which many had been subjected under the warriors' rule.

The mentality of intellectuals is fundamentally different from that of warriors or laborers. Unlike laborers, intellectuals are not inert or powerless in the face of obstacles.

But neither do they leap courageously into struggle as do those having the warrior mentality.

Instead, they first use their keen intellect to carefully devise a strategy of action. Then they put this strategy into effect by making use of the physical labor of the workers and the brute force and spirited courage of the warriors.

Their approach to action was not characterized by the drudgery of the laborers or the bold-spiritedness of the warriors, but by thoughtfulness and cunning.

Those who are mentally evolved have the capacity to direct their intellects towards genuine high-mindedness and to awaken spiritual awareness.

But the rule of intellectuals was rarely characterized by benevolence and true spirituality, for very few of them cultivated virtuous qualities. Instead, most of them used their mental gifts to fulfil their sensual desires.

In their efforts to get what they wanted, they avoided taking risks or doing any honest, hard work. Rather, the intelligentsia exploited the abilities of the laborers and warriors.

The intellectuals were adept at making an outward show of honesty and piousness.

But in their efforts to maintain their dominance and gratify their passions, there was no action too unscrupulous for them to undertake . . .

. . . And it was often difficult to discern the sinister intentions behind their cunning plans.

Unlike the warriors, whose path was simple and straightforward, the intellectuals were masters of deceit and could be crooked from start to finish.

Unfortunately for the public, both the ambition and the callousness of the intelligentsia frequently exceeded that of the power-thirsting monarchs of the prior warrior era.

The scale of the campaigns of conquest undertaken in the Age of Antiquity by the warrior class paled before the jihads and crusades of the Medieval Era instigated in the name of religion by the intellectual class.

Unlike the warriors, the intellectuals could not bully others through the use of brute force. So they needed some other method to compel people to respond to their bidding. Their most effective control was to cloud people's minds with religious dogmas, illogical superstitions, and bogus mythological stories. These were skillfully propagated to instill fear and inferiority into the minds of common people.

By this means, the intelligentsia kept people ignorant and were able to fill their minds with bigotry, fanaticism and blind faith.

This ignorance and religious fanaticism led to some of the darkest chapters in human history. When the priests launched their cruel inquisitions, millions of innocent people were burned at the stake by fear-ridden fanatics carrying out the "holy" work of the Church.

The clergy profited immensely from the false beliefs they sowed. People were led to believe that before they could receive the blessings of God they would have to petition those who were ordained to intervene on their behalf.

Only the priests, friars and mullahs could—for the right price—intercede with Vishnu, Jehovah or Allah to have the sins of the devout forgiven.

It was not possible for uneducated people in the Medieval Era to conceive of defying the God-sanctioned authority of the popes, ayatollahs and high priests.

Even the mighty kings and knights became the servants of the Church, believing without question that their crusades against the infidels would earn them glory in the coming kingdom of heaven.

The intellectual era did have a constructive side. To maintain their privileged position, the intellectuals preached religious philosophies; through this religious posturing society was benefited.

To convincingly pose as pillars of righteousness, the intelligentsia had to undertake public service. When they heard the religious discourses of the priests, the common people were often inspired to give attention to their moral and spiritual development. All this had a helpful effect on social progress.

The social system which evolved in the warrior era was based on firm discipline and collective unity.

In the intellectual era, society became more cohesive as religious teachings imparted a deeper sense of morality, leading to an increase in social awareness.

Whereas the warriors had their pyramids and palaces built by commanding slave labor to do their bidding, the great cathedrals and mosques of the intellectual era were built through the voluntary efforts of whole communities.

There was other good which came from the rule of intellectuals. Because of their talent for effectively administrating the society, people's abilities were put to fuller use. The material base of the society increased and, in general, people could better obtain their basic necessities.

People also enjoyed a greater degree of social security under the rule of the intelligentsia. Rather than being run by the dictates of royal whim—as it had been in the warrior age—government was more often run according to systems of law and constitutional authority.

35

Yet it cannot be said that the social edifice which was constructed in the intellectual era was built out of concern for people's needs or for their human sentiments. This was clearly evident in the institution of marriage. The families of the betrothed made the marriage arrangements without regard for the feelings of their children. Their primary concern was to maintain their family prestige and to preserve the rigidity of the class or caste system.

In the society of the intellectual era, women were severely oppressed. They lost their human dignity and were made wageless slaves and objects of men's enjoyment.

The church concocted scriptural injunctions—which were presented as divine commandments—declaring that a woman's role was to bear children and serve her man.

Because of this oppressive patriarchal dogma, a woman's very existence was defined in relation to men. Without a husband and children, a woman's life held little meaning in the eyes of society.

This caused women to develop crippling inferiority complexes and to suffer lives of great anguish and despair.

The priestly elite never shied away from taking full advantage of human weaknesses. They poisoned people's minds with pious scriptural utterances, typically spoken in dead languages.

They tormented people with fear, holding before them the prospect of dangling over the fires of hell should they fail to maintain blind adherence to the one true way to salvation.

In short, the society of the Middle Ages paid little regard to humanity. Religious dogmas were severely rigid and the social institutions were oppressive and inhumane.

But not all of the mentally developed people of that era were parasites on society. There were some noble-minded individuals who bravely struggled to humanize the social system. Great spiritual teachers, such as Gautama Buddha, Chuang Tzu, Francis of Assisi and Meister Eckhart sought to awaken humanity to the thrill of freedom, to dogma-free ways of thinking, and to the ideal of universal love.

These sages and saints were dearly loved by the common people, but were viciously attacked by those having vested interests to protect.

Many spiritually-inspired reformers were defamed, excommunicated or immolated for their so-called heretical teachings.

The intelligentsia would war against each other to establish the superiority of their contending doctrines. They exhibited intolerance of competing ideas and engaged in intense ideological clash.

But when any reformer tried to awaken rational and humanistic sentiments among the people, the leaders of the different sects would form unholy alliances to stop short the spread of progressive ideas. Establishment-defending intellectuals would fight humanistic reformers tooth and nail.

Sometimes the progressive ideas popularized by the martyred reformers gained acceptance. The intelligentsia would then praise these great people and use their memory in hypocritical oratories designed to further exploit the populace.

The intellectual class exhibited great cunning devoid of noble intent. They were inhuman, deceitful, rapacious, and—above all—selfish.

In the intellectual era, material wealth gradually assumed ever greater importance. With their intellects directed towards baser pursuits, the nobility and church officials indulged heavily in acquiring and enjoying refined material objects. They sought to expand their collections of art and finely crafted luxuries.

They also needed revenues to finance their war campaigns and crusades.

Although material wealth became important to the intelligentsia, they lacked the inclination and the practical skills to deal proficiently with commerce and finance. They had very little aptitude for barter and trade, for capital accumulation, for expansion of markets, or for money-lending.

The merchant class were adept at these commercial activities. Because of the nobility's growing desire for material commodities and the need to increase the state treasury, the status of the merchant class inevitably rose.

This development marked the twilight of the intellectual era and set the stage for another major change in class dominance.

Chapter Four

The Capitalist Era

The intelligentsia eventually found themselves dependent on merchants and financiers for monetary resources; this made them lose their position of social dominance. They were compelled to submit their formidable intellectual abilities to the service of those who controlled the economy.

The merchant class, through the force of their wealth, came to dominate the nobility, the clergy, and the professionals, as well as the warriors and the laborers.

Those whose mental tendency is to seek and amass wealth, and whose talent is to control the production and distribution of commodities, are known as capitalists. The period of history in which they hold dominance is called the capitalist era.

The growth in numbers of the capitalist class originated in the battle of wits during the intellectual era. There were losers in the struggle for intellectual prestige. Frequently, those who lost their stature as intellectuals sought some new means to establish their prestige in society.

Some of them directed their intellects towards the pursuit of making money. Engaging in finance and commerce did not carry the dignity of intellectual activities, but it did give them the command of the power of money.

Whereas intellectuals enjoy material objects through their use, capitalists enjoy wealth more through its possession. Their mental drive is to accumulate wealth, not necessarily to use it.

And, whereas the intellectuals would acquire their riches while maintaining an appearance of piety, the capitalists amassed their wealth in an open and straightforward manner.

Capitalists exhibit great courage in the course of their aggressive efforts to increase their worth. They bravely face many ups and downs in their fortune, and they take big economic risks as they daringly gamble their capital on opportunities for greater financial gain.

But, unlike the warriors, the capitalists do not maintain a sense of honor in their struggles. Their financial empire-building is undertaken without scruples or the inhibitions of moral codes.

For the sake of money, they are willing to compromise their character and to ignore the well-being of society.

There are some in the capitalist class who have enough conscience to be charitable. But they usually expect a return on their philanthropy through the enhancement of their public image.

The capitalist age began to emerge in Europe in the post-medieval era. This period saw the rapidly rising influence of powerful banking houses and the urban bourgeois. At this time the merchant class got the stagnant feudal economic order replaced by mercantilism.

Later, when the consolidation of their social dominance was complete, the laissez-faire economic system was introduced.

Simultaneous with the advent of the free-enterprise economy came the Industrial Revolution. By this point, the capitalists enjoyed unchallenged class dominance in most parts of Europe.

When the money-minded outlook of the capitalists becomes predominant in society, the individual's social value gets assessed in monetary terms. Money buys respect.

The capitalist era gave rise to nationalism. Behind the patriotic rhetoric of nationalism lay the capitalists' self-serving motive to gain control of strategic access to resources and to protect and extend markets.

The eventual and inevitable outgrowth of capitalistic nationalism was political and economic imperialism.

Imperialism led to the economic enslavement of colonized peoples. It also created a dangerous threat to global peace and unity.

The rivalries among the imperialist powers for access to resources and markets was the main cause of colonial wars, and of the brutally destructive world wars of this century.

The religious sentiments of the capitalist class tend to be based on fear of the Almighty. Their fear-based religiosity often compels them to engage in philanthropy to insure a prosperous afterlife.

But if—as often happens—they lose these religious inhibitions, then they become all the more unscrupulous and greedy in their pursuit of money.

The capitalist dominated society retained the system of male supremacy created in the intellectual era. Women continued to be deprived of their rightful social status and they became more economically dependent on men.

In the modern period of the capitalist era, liberalizing reforms have given women a measure of legal equality. But, for the most part, their second class economic condition continues.

The social codes and institutions of the intellectual era were mostly retained in the capitalist age. The governmental system, however, underwent substantial change. The capitalist class found that theocratic or monarchial rule was not responsive enough to their bidding. So they eventually adopted the democratic system of government.

Under democracy, people are easily deceived by the promises and propaganda of political leaders.

And politicians, in turn, are well aware of their dependence upon the moneyed class for contributions to their campaign coffers and for support of their governmental policies.

Democracy, however, does not always prove to be the best system for protecting capitalist interests. Should it become unwieldy for controlling mass unrest, it is expedient to replace it with dictatorial rule.

Not only in government, but in many other aspects of social life as well, intellectuals often play an important role in the capitalists' socio-economic system. Their intellectual abilities are essential to build a social order in which economic exploitation proceeds efficiently and with little public opposition.

Legislators frame laws advantageous to the propertied class. Diplomats negotiate trade agreements which protect corporate interests. Journalists write news reports conforming to the pro-business slant of the big publishers and media moguls.

Industrial psychologists devise more efficient production systems, and labor consultants skillfully devise ways to co-opt the demands of workers.

Political scientists, philosophers and theologians articulate theories which provide sophisticated justification for capitalism.

Authors and screen-writers churn out formula soap opera novels and banal TV and movie scripts which keep the public engrossed in escapist and mind-deadening fantasies.

Artists engage themselves in catering to the fancy of wealthy patrons or in providing advertising images to promote consumption.

Technicians and scientists invent destructive weapons for protecting the foreign investments of multinational corporations, or they develop new products or production systems which increase corporate profits.

Attorneys, professors and administrators also provide essential services to the capitalist class.

The courage and physical strength of the warrior class is similarly requisitioned to further capitalist interests.

Police are called upon to suppress militant labor unrest, and to infiltrate and spy on dissident groups.

The armed forces are sent into foreign lands to quell popular revolutionary movements. According to the disinformation campaigns of the political leaders, these military interventions are necessary to protect democracy.

But in reality it is the economic interests of the mega-banks and transnational corporations which are being protected.

For their loyal services, warrior heroes are honored with medals and words of praise. For their brilliant achievements, intellectual geniuses are awarded prizes and titles. Rewarded with a little money or reputation, the warriors and intellectuals continue to offer their heroic bravery, or their creative genius, in the service of the capitalist system.

Military personnel and professionals may be aware, to some extent, that they are prostituting themselves to the moneyed class. But they continue to accept their degradation because of self-interest, out of a lack of socio-economic consciousness, or because they need to earn a living.

Such subservience, however, is not universal. There are some moral-minded intellectuals and warriors who have strong humanistic values. They boldly speak out or take courageous action against exploitation.

But such dissent and agitation places these social activists in precarious situations. And because the risks of openly opposing capitalism are great, the number of activists generally remains few.

By efficiently marshalling the combined productive capacities of intellectuals, warriors and laborers, the capitalists bring about a great burst of technological and material advancement. In the capitalist dominated era, humanity produces unparalleled material abundance.

But humanity is also afflicted by great inequalities, rampant exploitation and desperate poverty. In addition, the earth is subjected to immense ecological destruction.

Greed-driven capitalists do not view the human society as an organism to be nurtured. Instead, society is regarded as a means to inflate their wealth through the sweat of the laborers, the intellect of the professionals, and the courage of the soldiers.

Rather than functioning in symbiotic unity with the other social classes, the capitalists live on the vital force of others. So intent can they become on building their financial empires that they devitalize—and may eventually kill—the very social organism on which they parasitically live.

Although most of the social ills of the capitalist era are owed to the effects of capitalist exploitation, the social respect enjoyed by the moneyed class is not easily tarnished.

This is because common people generally do not perceive the rapacious nature of the so-called free enterprise system. Nor do they readily comprehend its devastating effects on the environment, on society, and on the human mind.

Sometimes mass opposition to economic exploitation and social injustice arises to threaten the smooth functioning of capitalism. When sentiments for peace, justice, freedom, and anti-exploitation take hold among the populace, strikes, demonstrations, civil disobedience and active resistance break out.

To protect the status quo, the capitalist class has had to devise suitable means for blunting the force of social protest. Their most effective strategy is to keep people divided so they cannot perceive their common interests, and cannot attain the powerful unity they need to end their oppression. To implement their policy of divide and rule, the capitalist-subservient intellectuals introduce divisive ideologies and promote sentiments which encourage narrow self-interest.

The capitalists also patronize competing political parties, keeping political rivalries active. When stronger measures are necessary, scabs are recruited to break strikes and police forces are used to suppress labor, student and ethnic militancy. Through the compelling force of their money, the capitalists are able to engage the vitality of the warrior class and the cunning of the intellectual class to keep people ignorant, disunited, or suppressed.

But their drive to accumulate wealth creates increasingly miserable conditions for the general public—inflation, unemployment and poverty . . .

. . . pollution, urban decay, and environmental destruction . . .

... alienation, cultural decadence ...

... union busting, restrictions on civil liberties, police brutality ...

... and interventionist wars in support of brutal dictatorships. These unnatural conditions frustrate and oppress people's aspirations to enjoy a good life.

These conditions eventually become intolerable. The only alternative at that point is revolution against capitalist class domination.

Chapter Five

The Workers' Revolution

In the capitalist society, class relations are reduced to two groups: the capitalists, who control the means of production and distribution of wealth . . .

. . . and the laborers, warriors and intellectuals, who must sell their physical or mental labor to the capitalists. The workers, military, and professionals retain their distinctive mental characteristics; however, from an economic point of view, they become laborers. The revolution against capitalist rule is therefore called a workers' revolution.

There are many dissatisfied intellectuals and warrior-types who have been forced by economic circumstance into a laborer-like existence.

The leadership of a workers' revolution comes from the ranks of these disgruntled warrior-minded or intellectual-minded workers. The more humanistic and spirited of these courageously take a vanguard role in fostering the struggle for progressive reforms.

Those who are of laborer mentality generally are unable to express the courage and idealism necessary to take up the path of revolution. They do not perceive clearly the socio-economic and political causes of their difficulties; the thought of revolting does not readily enter their minds.

They endure their oppressed condition, concerned mainly for their day-to-day existence. Not until the disgruntled warrior/intellectual-minded workers inspire them with revolutionary visions, and not until their want becomes desperate enough, do they jump into the fray of struggle.

In order for a revolution to begin, it is not enough for the conditions of exploitation to be unbearably oppressive. For people to rise up in revolt, certain other conditions are also necessary. The oppressed must develop a revolutionary socio-economic theory which empowers them. They must overcome the influence of those religious beliefs which condition them to endure suffering, or which make them powerless to struggle for freedom.

People eventually realize that the benefits of the welfare state serve to pacify them and to reinforce a dependent mentality.

They begin to understand that establishing an exploitation-free society through purely democratic means is not a practical possibility while money controls the media and the electoral machinery.

And they finally stop expecting the moneyed class to be moved by reason and moral appeals to humanize the system. They realize that only discriminate and humane use of pressure can bring about the progressive society of their visions.

Competent leadership is another important necessity for the success of a workers' revolution. The leaders of a revolution cannot merely deliver stirring talks and rousing calls to action. They must also be well-disciplined, have a sacrificing spirit, be able to endure suffering, have a strong moral character, be capable of astute political analysis, and be able to conceive and carry out comprehensive strategies.

The path to victory in a workers' revolution does not proceed smoothly and directly; the struggle is bound to be a long one, full of set-backs and difficulties.

Those who unite to end exploitation will have to continually adjust to tactics devised by the dominant class to check the spread of revolutionary activity. They must see through the deceptions of the capitalist-controlled media.

They must be aware of the motives behind the psychological ploys and disinformation campaigns of the political leaders.

And they need to constantly revise their strategies in response to the state's increasingly repressive counter-measures.

The overthrow of capitalist domination requires force. A revolution can be conducted with little bloodshed, but only if a large portion of the revolutionaries are intellectual-minded.

If the warrior-minded revolutionaries dominate, then the struggle for freedom will be more violent.

Chapter Six

The Second Warrior Era

The first battles of the workers' revolution broke out in Western industrialized countries by the later part of the 19th Century. The first successful overthrow of capitalist domination occurred in the 1917 Bolshevik Revolution.

Post-capitalist societies have since been established in a number of other nations, most of them economically imperialized, developing countries.

The guiding political theory of most anti-capitalist revolutionary movements has been Marxism. It is a central belief of communism that, after the overthrow of the capitalist class, and under the subsequent dictatorship of the communist party, social classes will fade and a classless society will emerge.

But Marxist theory has proved inconsistent with historical reality. Rather, a new form of class oppression is tyrannizing people living in communist countries.

After the victory of the revolution, society passes out of the capitalist era and into a second laborer era. However, people with laborer mentality are not able to bring firm social order, or take control of social institutions, following the downfall of the capitalist state. The "proletariat" is simply not capable of leading the new society. For a short time there is social pandemonium.

Very soon—within a few hours, days or weeks—the warrior-minded leaders of the workers' revolution seize the state and impose martial order, ending the chaos. With the onset of their dictatorial leadership, the second warrior era begins.

This new warrior era is clearly evident in such post-capitalist societies as Nicaragua, Cuba, Vietnam, North Korea and Albania.

In the early period of the revolutionary society, the new warrior class shows some measure of humanitarian concern and effects needed social and economic reforms.

As a result, people gain security from economic want and enjoy a greater measure of socio-economic equality than they knew under capitalism.

But the militarist class eventually puts its own interests before the welfare of the people they rule. In the oppressive regimes they create, social life is regimented, freedom of thought is not tolerated, and religious worship is stifled.

Big centralized bureaucracies control the economy, social institutions and culture.

Artistic expression which is not in the state-sanctioned mold is suppressed. There is little to motivate entrepreneurs.

And even the glorified "proletariat" have little to cheer about. The rights of workers to organize independent unions is curtailed, basic consumer commodities are in short supply, and the workplace environment is as alienating as under capitalism.

If people try to speak out against the lack of human rights or the stagnant conditions in the militarist society, they are dealt with in a harsh manner by the ever-present internal security forces.

The militarist class maintains a large and powerful army, and it uses its armed forces to pursue its dreams of geo-political expansion or to suppress popular uprisings against the state. Funding for the development and deployment of their military might comes from the toil of the once sanctified laboring class.

Chapter Seven

The Second Intellectual Era

The creation and maintenance of a powerful state in the modern age requires the help of many trained technicians, well-educated professionals, and competent administrators. The military class, therefore, emphasizes the educational system to increase the numbers of intellectuals.

But it is these same intellectuals—scientists, artists, writers, educators—who feel most stifled in the society of the second warrior era. Even many of the younger, intellectual-minded party officials feel class conflict with the older, military-minded party bureaucrats. In the Soviet Union, Czechoslovakia, Poland, Hungary and China, dissident intellectuals have felt suppressed by warrior class domination, and have moved to end militarist rule.

They have demanded freedom of expression, democracy, and an end to centralized control of the economy. This political agitation marks the beginning of a transition to a new era in which the intelligentsia again dominates society. The first major revolt against militarist dominance came in Hungary in 1956. In 1968, a movement led by intellectuals began to take Czechoslovakian society into the next era. Both movements were crushed by Soviet military interventions. In 1980, the Solidarity union movement in Poland—supported and guided by the Church and dissident intellectuals—came close to moving Poland into the second intellectual era. But this forward movement of the social cycle was also forcefully suppressed.

In China in the early 1980s, a great internal power struggle resulted in a diminishing of military class influence. The generals of the People's Liberation Army who dominated the Communist Party Central Committee were removed. Old-guard, military-affiliated officials were purged and replaced by younger, intellectual-minded party members. China began to decentralize its economy, reduce the size and budget of its army, and allow greater freedom of cultural expression. This transition to a more open, intellectual-dominated society was blocked by the suppression of the pro-democracy movement in 1985 and by the brutal crushing of the 1989 student-led reform movement.

By 1987, the transition to the intellectual era began to shake the Soviet Union. *Glasnost* and *perestroika*—policies conceived and supported by the intellectual class—have brought profound social, economic and political reforms. Militarist influence is on the wane.

In Poland and Hungary, political party pluralism is being restored; the movement to a new intellectual era is even more consolidated.

The new intelligentsia beginning to take leadership in Poland, Hungary and Russia are clearly reform-minded. Their restructuring of society is bringing increased openness in government, greater scope for individual expression, more efficiency in the economy, and a lessening of cultural regimentation. However, it is unlikely that their rule will maintain its progressive direction.

While the new leaders identify with their own class interests, they will inevitably apply their brilliant minds to rule society to their advantage. The tyranny of the warrior class will be replaced by the tyranny of the intellectual class. Again, the bane of class oppression will afflict society.

Chapter Eight

Sadvipras

History has shown that one class inevitably follows another in a regular succession of class dominance. The second capitalist era will follow the now-developing second intellectual era. Capital accumulation will again become the all-consuming motive force of society.

And when capitalist exploitation proves too burdensome, there will be a new period of revolutionary upheaval, advancing society into the third round of the social cycle.

This rotation of the social cycle is the natural flow of class dynamics. It happens according to natural social law, and none can check its advance. For this reason, the classless society promised by Marxism has proved to be an utopian dream. But this does not mean that class tyranny is our unavoidable fate.

Class mentality will continue to exist; it is deeply rooted in human psychology. The rotation of the social cycle will continue. Yet, it is possible for the social cycle to advance to a new era before stagnancy and class exploitation set in. In the view of philosopher P.R. Sarkar, humanity's ability to keep the social cycle progressively advancing will depend upon the existence of a large number of classless people called *sadvipras*.

Sadvipras are spiritually evolved personalities who possess self-discipline, mental determination, rational judgment, uncompromising moral principles, and great compassion for humanity.

They operate from an internalized realization of the unity and interconnectedness of all existence. This spiritual vision imbues them with a profound love for all life.

Sadvipras appreciate and cultivate the abilities of all the social classes. They can serve humanity through physical labor. They have the courage to struggle for social good, the intellect to guide social progress, and the finesse to promote economic development. Being without class identification, they do not hesitate to fight against any form of class exploitation.

Sadvipras will keep in close touch with the conditions and aspirations of common people and will vigilantly observe the flow of social evolution.

When they see that people's welfare and expression are being unnaturally checked because of exploitation by the dominant class, they will take the lead in the struggle to oust this class from power and advance the social cycle into the next era.

To bring about progressive movement in a stagnating society, they will make people aware of their rights. They will challenge the false dogmas used to justify oppressive conditions, and they will make whatever sacrifice is necessary to insure that humanity's dynamic momentum is not hindered.

Sadvipras will perform an important role. They will create a firm moral and spiritual foundation for society, and they will work with dedication for the all-round emancipation of human beings and the protection of non-human life.

Sadvipra-like personalities have existed in the past, but they have been few. A profound cultural transformation is now in progress; a new era is about to be born. This transformation will establish universal human values at the core of our social life. An enlightened world culture will arise, out of which many sadvipras will emerge. Indeed, their emergence is already in progress.

With the help of sadvipras, the human story will continue. A liberated humanity will soon reach out towards now undreamed-of heights of achievement.

About the Authors

Ronald Logan wrote the text for *HumanStory*. Ron has a master's degree in counseling and is a long-time student of Prout (Progressive Utilization Theory), the socio-economic theory of Indian renaissance philosopher P.R. Sarkar. Ron's books include *The Cosmic Society* and *Prout: a New Ideology for a New Era*. Ron lives in Eugene, Oregon with his daughter, Melissa, who shares her father's love for the wild and natural.

Michael McClure illustrated and designed *HumanStory*. Mike is an artist who lives with his wife and three children in the Ozark Mountains of southern Missouri. He has been a student of P.R. Sarkar since 1972, and delights in bringing together the ridiculous and the sublime.

Your views, comments, and questions about *HumanStory* or Prout can be directed to the authors through the publisher's address.

On the following pages, write and draw your own script for the 1990's. What will happen? What will the New Age be like? How will it arrive— quietly or with a bang? What part will you play? Let yourself go, have fun, and if you like—send us a copy of your creation. We'd love to see it!

The authors